THE COMPLETE BOOK OF SHOES

THE COMPLETE BOOK OF SHOES

MARTA MORALES

A FIREFLY BOOK

Published by Firefly Books Ltd. 2013

Copyright © 2013 LOFT Publications

First printing

Publisher Cataloging-in-Publication Data (U.S.)

A CIP record for this title is available from the Library of Congress

Library and Archives Canada Cataloguing in Publication

A CIP record for this title is available from Library and Archives Canada

Published in the United States by
Firefly Books (U.S.) Inc.
P.O. Box 1338, Ellicott Station
Buffalo, New York 14205

Published in Canada by
Firefly Books Ltd.
50 Staples Avenue, Unit 1
Richmond Hill, Ontario L4B 0A7

Printed in China

Acknowledgments

I would like to thank each of the selected designers, as well as the agencies that represent them, for their participation in this project. Their contributions have been vital to understanding the art of the shoe, and this book would not have been possible without them.

Every page is dedicated to Eloy and Maria José, my parents. Their unconditional support and affection have made me everything I am.

This title was developed by
LOFT Publications
Via Laietana, 32 4th fl. of. 92
08003 Barcelona, España
Tel.: +34 93 268 80 88
Fax: +34 93 268 70 73
loft@loftpublications.com
www.loftpublications.com

For Loft:
Editorial coordinator: Claudia Martínez Alonso
Assistant to editorial coordinator: Ana Marques
Editor and textw: Marta Morales
Art director: Mireia Casanovas Soley
Cover layout: Emma Termes Parera
Layout: Cristina Simó Perales
Translation: textcase

"Give a girl the right pair of shoes and she can conquer the world," American actress Bette Midler once said. Her words reveal the power of shoes to transform a woman's personality and look, a woman who makes an impression thanks to the femininity and comfort that she gets from wearing a good pair of shoes.

Who could forget the tale of Cinderella? A girl loses a glass slipper at a ball, and after getting it back from her prince, she dons the shoe and transforms from a humble servant girl into a beautiful princess. The same happens in real life because shoes have that magical touch that can change a look completely. And who could fail to notice the passion that so many celebrities have for shoes? Perhaps one of the most famous examples is Imelda Marcos, the former First Lady of the Philippines, who actually accumulated more than 1,000 pairs of shoes over the 20 years her husband was in power.

Shoes have undeniably become beautiful objects of desire, and many of them are veritable works of art. This book showcases some of the most innovative, elegant, seductive and ingenious designs from 40 select brands. Each designer has a unique way of envisioning the art of the shoe, and though their styles may differ, they all have one thing in common: a passion and irrepressible weakness for these items of beauty. The sentiment that unites them is expressed by the use of top quality materials, meticulous design and, of course, attention to detail.

The designers and fashion companies that appear in this book have a distinct style of their own, which guarantees their place at the vanguard of the footwear industry. To be precise, they were chosen for their innovative approach to design, their unerring focus on quality and their amazing artistry. The skill shown in each of their creations characterizes today's footwear industry and will undoubtedly influence its future trends.

Originally created as a protective cover for the feet, shoes have evolved to become veritable gems to be shown off with every step we take. In the past, making or repairing shoes was considered a humble trade, comparable to that of carpenters, blacksmiths or seamstresses. However, the relentless pace of today's footwear industry means that a handcrafted shoe has become a prized item created by highly skilled professionals.

The variety of shoe styles available today enables individuals to fully express their individual tastes at any time of day and within any culture. Shoes are actually the perfect accessory. They are available as flats, platforms, stilettos, classical and avant-garde styles as well as elegant, vintage, retro, groundbreaking, and experimental styles. The list is endless, and choosing the right shoe is essential in shaping the ultimate look for anyone who chooses their footwear mindfully.

The future of shoe design is unquestionably in the hands of contemporary designers, such as those included in this book, who express their identity in each of their creations. Although their shoe designs are different, they all share the common thread of exquisite craftsmanship.

Futurism and irreverence prevail in every shoe crafted by Anastasia Radevich. The Belarus-born Canadian designer challenges gravity and physics with her highly creative personal style. After being chosen as the best emerging designer at the London Festival Design in 2009, this artist has had a non-stop run of success. Despite her youth, Anastasia Radevich can already boast of having spent two years working with ALDO Shoes, Alexander McQueen and Nicholas Kirkwood, truly avant-garde designers

ANASTASIA RADEVICH

whose innovative and unconventional spirit she has managed to absorb. Mixing organic materials and mechanical shapes and using advanced technological processes, such as 3-D printing, this designer creates uniquely sculptured shoes. Clear proof of this can be seen in her Biofuture (2009), Kinetik (2010), Dreamfall (2011) and Lost Civilizations (2012) collections. There is no doubt that the originality of her shoes has firmly established her as one of the boldest and most unique creators in today's fashion scene.

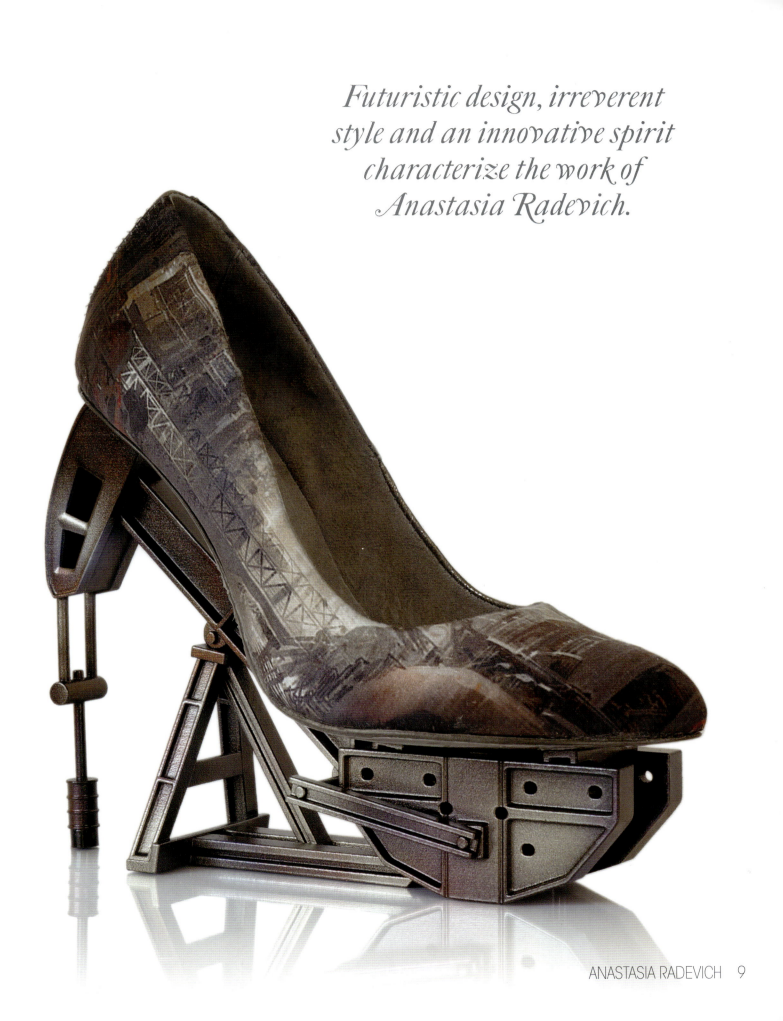

Futuristic design, irreverent style and an innovative spirit characterize the work of Anastasia Radevich.

Ra

Shoe created from leather,
metal and bronze
(Lost Civilizations collection, 2012).

Isis
Leather, metal and ABS plastic shoe
(Lost Civilizations collection, 2012).

Lotus
Leather, plastic and metal shoe
(Lost Civilizations collection, 2012).

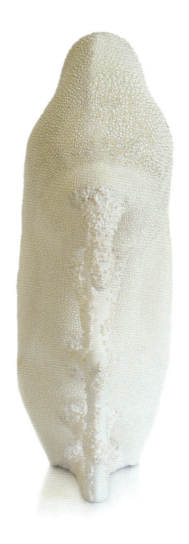 

The Work of Nature
Plastic and metal shoe with
fish scale engraving
(Lost Civilizations collection, 2012).

Ankle boot made with leather and lace with black metal heel (Kinetik collection, 2010).

Embossed leather sandal
with black metal heel
(Kinetik collection, 2010).

April
Ankle boot made of leather,
silk, plastic and metal
(Dreamfall collection, 2011).

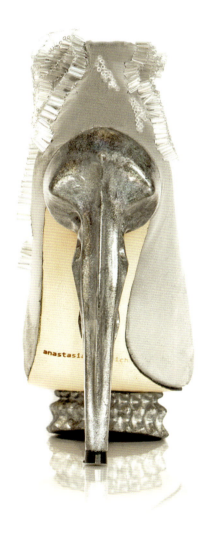

Kian
Ankle boot made of leather,
silk and ABS plastic
(Dreamfall collection, 2011).

Neverland
Ankle boot with screen-printed silk
(Lost Civilizations collection, 2012).

This Will Destroy You, Black Force
Black ankle boot with
Swarovski crystals
(Lost Civilizations collection, 2012).

Aperlaï is a French line of luxury accessories founded in 2009 by Alessandra Lanvin (a former headhunter in Paris' luxury sector). Pure lines, contrasts, asymmetry and sophistication are the values that shape this brand's style. Aperlaï's shoe designs are brought to fruition by the hands of top craftsmen near Venice, in Italy. With its varied palette of bright colors, Aperlaï's creations hark back to the works of painters like Joan Miró, Alexander Calder, Pablo Picasso and Piet Mondrian. Each shoe is designed

APERLAÏ

so that its colors define the boundaries of its shape; vibrant colors are embedded in suggestive curves, sharp lines, unexpected crisscrossing and outrageously high heels. Each design uses textures that are refined and simple, such as velvety suede, exotic leather, trim, soft textures and metallic reflections. Their shoes also feature fine details such as hidden leather linings and buttons, as well as mixed textures. Shine and mirror effects on the heels add a festive touch to the firm's latest collections. With surreal harmony, Aperlaï's shoes exude a simple, refined charm.

With surrealistic harmony,
Aperlaï's shoes exude a simple,
refined charm.

Geisha
Leather sandal with
graphic rectangular heel
(Spring-Summer 2012).

Spoky
Leather sandal
(Spring-Summer 2012).

Demi Circle

Leather sandal with
graphic rectangular heel
(Spring-Summer 2012).

Half
Leather asymmetrical sandal
(Spring-Summer 2012).

Tris
Blue leather court shoe
(Spring-Summer 2012).

Spokette
Fuchsia leather court shoe
(Spring-Summer 2012).

Circle

Mixed material shoe with inner platform and graphic heel (Fall-Winter 2011-2012).

Omega
Leather sandal with graphic heel
(Spring-Summer 2012).

Geisha doll

Velvet court shoe with rectangular marble-effect heel (Fall-Winter 2012-2013).

Baby brick
Black suede sandal with red fur trim
(Fall-Winter 2011-2012).

Shapes

Suede court shoe with
inner platform and graphic heel
(Fall-Winter 2011-2012).

Spok
Two-toned suede ankle boot
(Fall-Winter 2011-2012).

Armour
Blue and black suede ankle boot
(Fall-Winter 2011-2012).

Birdie
Suede and pony skin
ankle boot inspired by
the work of painter Joan Miró
(Fall-Winter 2012-2013).

Catalan bootie
Suede and velvet ankle boot
(Fall-Winter 2012-2013).

Pollock
Suede and leather ankle boot inspired
by the work of Jackson Pollock
(Fall-Winter 2012-2013).

Thanks to her French-Vietnamese heritage, French designer Barbara Bui finds inspiration for her collections in a global concept of urban cool. Her designs exude elegance, energy and sensitivity, with a huge dose of femininity thrown in for good measure. Sensual silhouettes, modern lines and precious materials permeate each of her shoe designs. Barbara Bui's trademark is total freedom to experiment with textures, decorations and materials. Elegance and boldness go hand in hand for this designer, as

BARBARA BUI

demonstrated by her colorful, sophisticated ankle boots with their combination of multicolored strass with leather and natural fur, as well as her discreet, elegant *prêt-à-porter* court shoes. From Paris to New York, Moscow to Dubai, her brand is highly praised among fashion lovers. So far, celebrity fans include Rosie Huntington-Whiteley, Zoe Saldana, Evan Rachel Wood, Lake Bell, Jessica Alba, Rachel Weisz and Rachel Zoe.

*Elegance and boldness go hand
in hand for Barbara Bui.*

Python print sandal
(Spring-Summer 2012).

Green and white high-heeled
sandal with ankle strap
(Spring-Summer 2012).

High-heeled blue suede
court shoe with gold trim
(Fall-Winter 2012-2013).

Black and gold leather sandal
(Fall-Winter 2012-2013).

Brown ankle boot sandal
with plaited leather
(Spring-Summer 2008).

Black leather open-toed ankle boot
with lace and python print
(Spring-Summer 2009).

Black suede ankle boot with embroidered snakes (Fall-Winter 2012-2013).

Gem-encrusted ankle boot
with silver embroidery
(Fall-Winter 2011-2012).

Leopard print ankle boot
with wedge heel
(Fall-Winter 2006-2007).

Flannel, rawhide and
sheepskin ankle boot
(Fall-Winter 2010-2011).

Black leather wedge
ankle boot with buckles
(Fall-Winter 2006-2007).

Black suede wedge
ankle boot with side zip
(Fall-Winter 2011-2012).

In 2010, Paco Gil's company Moda Elda launched the BF Colección Europa brand, a 100% made-in-Spain brand that is designed by a group of young artists including Paco Gil Jr. and Carla Gil. The collaboration is the perfect creative team for BF Colección Europa, and the result is a whimsical collection where objects of desire and unique pieces are abundant. Originality, freshness and fun are the foundations upon which this brand builds its creations. BF Colección Europa is characterized by its high-quality

BF COLECCIÓN EUROPA

finishes, and its company philosophy places great importance on luxury and extravagance. Founded to satisfy a woman's desire to emanate glamor and to feel good about herself, the feminine look of the shoes help to define their distinct style. Each creation is designed with precision, while maintaining a fresh, vibrant feel. BF Colección Europa shoes are ideal for women who don't want to go unnoticed, who care for their appearance down to the finest detail and who find pleasure in adorning their feet.

Fun, innovative designs characterize the
BF Colección Europa shoe line.

Bibian

Vinyl peep toe court shoe with heel, platform and kiwi-colored edging. Inspired by the tropics. Straight acrylic-glass heel with multicolored feathers inside and printed on the maxi-bow (Spring-Summer 2011).

Vovony

T-strap sandal made of fuchsia printed microfiber fabric with pink, black, yellow and orange details on a white background. Fuchsia suede back. Funnel-shaped platform heel painted in a tortoiseshell design (Spring-Summer 2012).

Golf

Court shoe with concealed platform made of red and black leopard print suede, decorated with tiny aged silver studs (Fall-Winter 2010-2011).

Midtail

Round toe court shoe in an extravagant burgundy-tone print with a bow at the toe (Fall-Winter 2012-2013).

Milla

Peep toe slingback sandal made of transparent vinyl and black-and-white polka dot fabric. Black patent leather edging and platform with medium height Plexiglas block heel housing another heel covered with matching polka dot fabric (Spring-Summer 2012).

Zaira

Ankle boot with stiletto heel in a combination of printed leathers, black suede and sequins, with silver glitter and precious stone trim (Fall-Winter 2010-2011).

Kilmore

Black napa stiletto court shoe with matching maxi-bow on the side (Fall-Winter 2011-2012).

Bonbon

High-heeled black suede court shoe with concealed platform over silver-laminated leather. Red patent leather lips motif with mini rhinestones (Fall-Winter 2010-2011).

Riga

Ankle boot with smoked
Plexiglas heel, rounded
leather toe and silver glitter
(Fall-Winter 2012-2013).

Nivea
Black suede ankle boot with medium heel and textile mesh peppered with glitter trim. Back zip closure (Fall-Winter 2010-2011).

Manhattan

Leopard print pony skin ankle boot with elastic on the side. Maxi heel and platform covered in matching wood (Fall-Winter 2011-2012).

Gila 2
Ankle boot with rounded toe, tapered heel and mix of leather and patent leather. Inner zip fastening (Fall-Winter 2012-2013).

Umbria

Tall boot with flat heel in brown leather embossed with a flower pattern combined with smooth leather with gold studs. Small decorative strap, gold trim at the ankle and inner zip (Fall-Winter 2012-2013).

Fulham

Tall boot with round toe in zebra print black suede and pony skin. Zip outer closure (Fall-Winter 2011-2012).

The trademark of the Caramelo brand is its ability to design different types of shoes for any time of day without sacrificing style or comfort. Over a span of 40 years in the industry, Caramelo has gained ground as one of the leading Spanish fashion companies and has established its own style based on quality, elegance and comfort. The brand views fashion as a form of expression, a commitment to its clients and a way of life.

CARAMELO

This philosophy is reflected in every shoe; each pair successfully blends classicism and modernism with a functional yet elegant design. The key to its success lies in the way it captures the essence of urban life with flair and grace, positioning itself at the vanguard of fashion and footwear trends with its simple, timeless designs. With more than 800 points of sale around the world, the company continues to evolve with each season in order to meet the needs of the market and rise to new challenges.

Caramelo shoes blend classicism and modernism with functional yet elegant design.

Peep toe court shoe reminiscent of the past. Caramelo by Antonio Pernas (Spring-Summer 2011).

Suede and leather
dance hall-style shoe
(Spring-Summer 2010).

Suede sandal with medium height heel and decorative stones (Spring-Summer 2008).

Snakeskin embossed leather sandal
(Spring-Summer 2010).

Jute wedge yellow fabric sandal
(Spring-Summer 2011).

High-heeled knotted leather sandal
(Spring-Summer 2011).

Satin and suede two-toned peep toe
court shoe with ankle strap
(Fall-Winter 2010-2011).

Red suede wedge
(Spring-Summer 2010).

Suede ankle sandal with
whimsical cut-outs and high heel.
Caramelo by Antonio Pernas
(Spring-Summer 2011).

 Suede peep toe in contrasting tones (Fall-Winter 2008-2009).

High-heeled satin and leather
sandal with tie on the heel.
Caramelo by Antonio Pernas
(Fall-Winter 2011-2012).

 High-heeled peep toe sandal
in suede and satin
(Fall-Winter 2009-2010).

Suede and leather
court shoe with studs
(Fall-Winter 2012-2013).

Leather loafer with
wooden platform and heel
(Fall-Winter 2009-2010).

High-heeled ankle boot
with visible fur lining
(Fall-Winter 2011-2012).

High-heeled ankle boot with invisible platform and suede fringe (Fall-Winter 2012-2013).

The origins of Castañer date back to 1776, when the first espadrille maker in the family was born: Rafael Castañer. The company that exists today, evolved from a tiny workshop, was founded in 1927 by Luis Castañer and his cousin Tomás Serra. Castañer has survived many ups and downs, such as the Spanish Civil War in 1936, when it was nationalized; its product was considered to be of military interest, as the soldiers sent to the front wore espadrilles. The company suffered financial difficulties in the

CASTAÑER

1950s when the famous Chiruca brand began using vulcanized rubber on soles to make them last longer. In the late 1970s, Lorenzo and Isabel Castañer (the next generation) met Yves Saint Laurent, who commissioned them to make the first wedge-heeled espadrille in history. This major innovation heralded an upturn for the brand by turning this peasant shoe into a luxury fashion must-have that looked perfect on the catwalk. Since then, Castañer has also attracted the attention of other first-rate fashion houses, including Hermès, Louis Vuitton and Christian Louboutin.

Castañer turned the humble espadrille into a luxury fashion must-have that looks perfect on the catwalk.

Hena

Patchwork fabric espadrille with wedge heel dyed red and fuchsia (Spring-Summer 2012).

Fiona
Orange fabric sandal with leather trim and wooden wedge heel (Spring-Summer 2011).

Edita

Red satin sandal with flower trim and jute wedge heel (Spring-Summer 2011).

Eloise
Red and white platform wedge
espadrille with ankle strap
(Spring-Summer 2011).

Kika

Red satin wedge peep toe sandal with ankle strap and gold studs (Spring-Summer 2011).

Lisa

Red satin sandal
with poppy on one side
(Spring-Summer 2010).

Lisa

Mauve velvet Mary Jane with gray
wedge heel, buckle and button trim
(Fall-Winter 2011-2012).

Bibian
Navy satin peep toe sandal
with purple espadrille and sequin
trim on the upper
(Spring-Summer 2012).

Millicent
Khaki suede sandal
with straps and jute platform
(Fall-Winter 2009-2010).

Yoyo
Retro golden sandal with block heel
(Fall-Winter 2012-2013).

Krista
Clog-style chocolate suede sandal
with wooden heel and platform
(Fall-Winter 2011-2012).

Fusta
Cognac lace-up shoe
with beige suede wedge
(Fall-Winter 2010-2011).

Cesare Paciotti shoes not only feature elegant, contemporary shapes, they also have the ability to transform any look with a touch of glamor and sophistication. Born in Civitanova Marche, Italy, Paciotti's passion for shoes stems from a family tradition passed down by his parents, who had owned a shoe company since 1948. He went on to perfect his artistic talent at the prestigious DAMS (music, art and performing arts) graduate studies program at the University of Bologna. After many trips around the world, which helped

CESARE PACIOTTI

fine-tune his creativity, in 1980 he took over the company's creative design and renamed it Cesare Paciotti. His designs blend outstanding craftsmanship with an impeccable use of accessories. Cesare Paciotti shoes are designed for strong, sophisticated and modern women, as reflected in all of his collections. The brand's logo, which is stamped onto the soles of its shoes, is a dagger — meant to symbolize power and tradition, values that are unquestionably present in every detail on Cesare Paciotti's luxurious shoes.

"Shoes embody the art of seduction." — Cesare Paciotti

Twiggy

Colorful mosaic-patterned
suede court shoe with a high heel,
inspired by the 1970s
(Fall-Winter 2008-2009).

Butterfly

Shoe inspired by the weightlessness of a butterfly's flight. The colors, embroidery, lace and transparencies symbolize the wings, while the thick heel represents its body (Spring-Summer 2009).

Beatrice

High-heeled court shoe
with turquoise trim
(Spring-Summer 2008).

Courtney
Court shoe inspired by the
rock and roll lifestyle depicted by
vintage T-shirts and their fabrics
(Spring-Summer 2008).

Carla

Gray suede lace-up shoe with brocade fabric across silky white leather toe (Fall-Winter 2008-2009).

Essence
Brown ankle boot with
tassel trim on the heel
(Fall-Winter 2011-2012).

Galaxy

Boot with a waterfall of Swarovski crystals of varying sizes (Fall-Winter 2007-2008).

Queen of the Snow

Mink-covered boot with pearls, satin bows, Swarovski crystals and flowers reminiscent of the snow (Fall-Winter 2006-2007).

@Cnica
Black, gray and red ethnic-style shoe
(Spring-Summer 2008).

Dance in Versailles
Gray court shoe with flowers and brocade, a tribute to French Queen Marie Antoinette (Spring-Summer 2007).

Albert

Black court shoe with high heel and gold edges blending masculine and feminine styles. A tribute to the film *Albert Nobbs* (Fall-Winter 2012-2013).

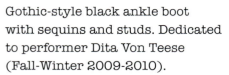

Dita
Gothic-style black ankle boot with sequins and studs. Dedicated to performer Dita Von Teese (Fall-Winter 2009-2010).

Chie Mihara is a brand with multicultural influences that are clearly a reflection of the designer's roots. Born in Porto Alegre, in Brazil, to Japanese parents, Chie Mihara studied fashion design at Kyushu University in Japan, followed by accessories design at New York's Fashion Institute of Technology. In 2001, she ventured out on her own, creating the brand Chie Mihara; a purveyor of shoes designed by and for women, which she launched in the Spanish city of Elda, Alicante. Mihara's designs are in-

CHIE MIHARA

spired by multicultural memories and experiences from her past: Brazil lends them a feminine, colorful touch; Japan influences their creator's approach to design; New York contributes to their functionality; and Spain is the source of their superior craftsmanship. Mihara designs shoes that are visually and emotionally attractive with a practical, artisan aspect. Each of her models is a quality product that prioritizes comfort and design.

*Chie Mihara's goal is to create
shoes that are feminine,
fun and comfortable.*

Bantus
Multicolored suede
and snakeskin print sandal
(Spring-Summer 2012).

Roger
Multicolored leather, goatskin
suede and embossed leather sandal
(Spring-Summer 2012).

Iona

Goatskin leather shoe with patterned leather-covered heel (Spring-Summer 2010).

Pinpon
Multicolored leather
and goatskin suede shoe
(Fall-Winter 2012-2013).

Edesa

Platform lace-up sandal in mustard
yellow cowhide with cork heel
(Spring-Summer 2011).

Sullivan
Leather and goatskin suede lace-up
shoe (Fall-Winter 2011-2012).

Séptimo

Cowhide and black goatskin shoe with ostrich skin effect (Fall-Winter 2011-2012).

Foreso
Multicolored leather and goatskin suede lace-up shoe (Fall-Winter 2011-2012).

Taiko
Navy leather sandal
(Spring-Summer 2011).

Átame
Lambskin shoe with bow trim
(Fall-Winter 2009-2010).

Founded in 1978 by Giacomo Mazzieri in the Italian town of Sala Baganza, near Parma, Coccinelle has become a prestigious shoe, accessory and bag brand. In Italian, *coccinelle* means "ladybug," and this lucky beetle is not only the brand's name, it is its mascot as well. Attention to detail, quality, simplicity and the latest trends are distinctive features of Coccinelle products. Their range of shoes suits the tastes of all women and are great for any time of day, spanning from ballet flats to wedge sandals to sky-

COCCINELLE

high heels. Each Coccinelle shoe is designed in keeping with the original traditions of Italian craftsmanship, using sensible but stylish details through the use of fine materials. Constant investment in research and technology ensures that the brand's collections have an innovative, elegant and modern feel. Sophistication, design and quality are the trademarks of each Coccinelle shoe, crafted with the total dedication of expert artisans.

In Italian, coccinelle *means "ladybug," and this lucky beetle is also the brand's mascot.*

Flat gladiator suede sandal
with decorative gemstones
(Spring-Summer 2011).

Flat purple suede sandal
with decorative gemstones
(Spring-Summer 2011).

Ostrich skin moccasin-style
court shoe with gray flocking
(Fall-Winter 2011-2012).

Python sandal with ankle strap and suede wedge (Spring-Summer 2011).

Oxford leather shoe in brown tones
(Fall-Winter 2011-2012).

Masculine yellow lace-up shoe
(Spring-Summer 2012).

Studded gray suede ankle boot
(Fall-Winter 2009-2010).

  Gray leather ankle boot
with crocodile back and heel
(Fall-Winter 2012-2013).

Black leather biker-style ankle boot
(Fall-Winter 2009-2010).

Flat masculine ankle boot
with elastic inserts on the side
(Fall-Winter 2012-2013).

Flat gray suede boot
with fold-over at the top
(Fall-Winter 2009-2010).

Brown leather boot with back zip
(Fall-Winter 2012-2013).

Tall leather boot with fold-over at the top and wedge heel (Fall-Winter 2009-2010).

Tall black leather boot
metallic block heel
(Fall-Winter 2011-2012).

Tall black leather boot with crocodile back and heel (Fall-Winter 2012-2013).

Flat riding boot with the company's logo embossed in the leather (Fall-Winter 2012-2013).

Born in the Spanish town of Elche, Alicante, which is home to a prominent leather tanning and footwear industry, Antonia (Toñi) Pastor created Cuplé in 1987. Her brand targets a discerning audience for whom a balance between quality and fashion is paramount. Collections brimming with originality have arisen from her grand aesthetic vision and perennial need to innovate. Her shoes are remarkable for their variety and the uniqueness of their design. Cuplé's footwear and leather goods are manufactured in

CUPLÉ

the Spanish province of Alicante in its own workshops and also by partner companies. This enables Cuplé to maintain complete control over the entire creative process (from conception to packaging), ensuring added value. Whenever the design permits, the brand uses pink as an emblem of style and femininity. Cuplé's shoes have been worn on catwalks in Spain and abroad, accessorizing the collections of designers like Mercedes de Miguel, Dolores Cortés, Hannibal Laguna, Antonio Alvarado and Juan Duyos.

Cuplé shoes provide a touch of style and glamor for women who remain elegant all day long.

Leather Mary Jane in
black, orange and beige
(Fall-Winter 2012-2013).

Orange suede court shoe with
decorative trim on the back and
black block heel
(Fall-Winter 2012-2013).

Gray suede ankle boot with red bow
(Fall-Winter 2010-2011).

Red reptile skin-effect
court shoe with suede toe
(Spring-Summer 2011).

Purple velvet strappy sandal
(Fall-Winter 2010-2011).

Blue leather strappy sandal
studded with crystals on the heel
(Fall-Winter 2010-2011).

Bright blue sandal with
crossover black-edged straps
(Fall-Winter 2012-2013).

Blue suede Mary Jane court shoe with black strap (Fall-Winter 2012-2013).

Three-toned sandal (white, gold and camel) with ankle strap (Spring-Summer 2012).

Gold court shoe with
large brooch at the toe
(Spring-Summer 2011).

Reptile print court shoe
(Spring-Summer 2011).

Leopard print court shoe
(Fall-Winter 2011-2012).

Black suede sandal
with straps and chains
(Fall-Winter 2010-2011).

  Leather lace-up studded sandal
(Spring-Summer 2010).

Masculine black
lace-up sequined shoe
(Fall-Winter 2010-2011).

Tapestry-covered masculine
lace-up shoe with black suede toe
(Fall-Winter 2010-2011).

Spanish company Deux Souliers has been providing shoes with their trademark modernity, quality and handcraftsmanship since 2010. The brand's artistic director, Nunu Solsona, stresses the quest for balance between contrasting concepts such as traditional craftsmanship and avant-garde, while also paying attention to the tiniest details, such as decorative seams, specially worked leathers and hand painting. The result? Unique, timeless shoes of the most exquisite quality. From the company's inception,

DEUX SOULIERS

the objective behind the designs has been to craft comfortable, sustainable, high-quality shoes. This brand's collections feature organic and minimalistic lines; a style closely tied to their creator's way of thinking, as she has always believed that a shoe should last a lifetime in terms of durability and design. Deux Souliers provides a reliable range of products; contemporary updates of the classics crafted with fine, high-quality materials, with added artisan touches and assembly methods to ensure durability.

Moving forward is as simple as putting one foot in front of the other. A pair of shoes is all you need. This is the Deux Souliers slogan.

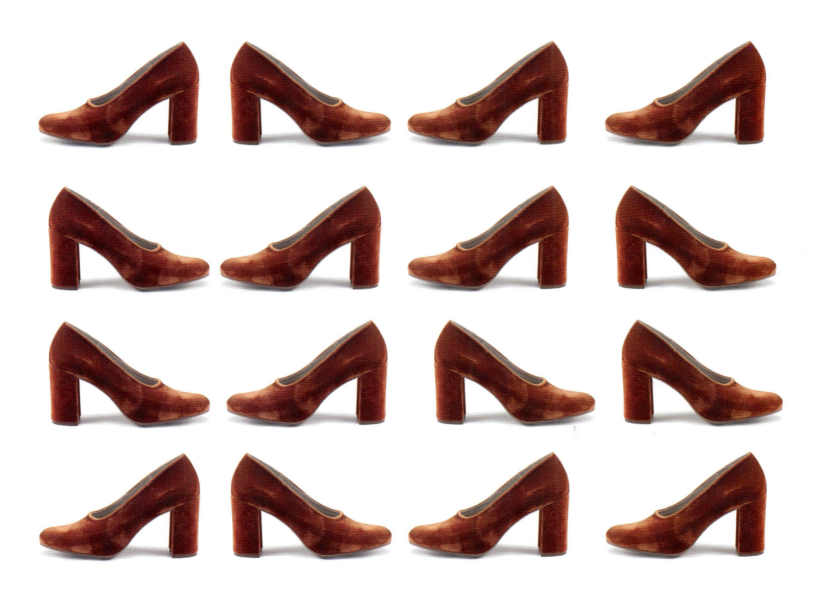

Buckle Heel #1

High block heel shoe with adjustable straps and buckles. Sides of buffed calfskin with nickel-plated hardware (Spring-Summer 2012).

Tongue Heel #1
Peep toe lace-up shoe with
tongue and leather sole
(Spring-Summer 2012).

Moccasin #1 Brown

Brown moccasin with
flat cork platform
(Spring-Summer 2012).

Buckle Moccasin #2
Moccasin with straight cork platform and buckle. Gray-blue cowhide and pumpkin color felt upper (Fall-Winter 2012-2013).

Oxford #1 Biscuit

Masculine fabric and calfskin shoe
with hand-painted contrasting edges
(Spring-Summer 2012).

Slipper #1
Geometric slip-on with
contrasting elastic inserts
(Spring-Summer 2012).

Clog #1
Closed toe clog with wood-covered
platform and overlapping leather
straps on the uppers and sole
(Spring-Summer 2012).

Flat #1 black

Black patent leather and calfskin
ballet flat with leather sole and
microporous rubber sole
(Fall-Winter 2012-2013).

Diego Dolcini's shoes are veritable sculptures; objects that evoke desire, achieve equilibrium between differing heights and streamline designs by using high-quality materials. His collections draw inspiration from the worlds of art, cinema and architecture. The women who wear his shoes become more beautiful by the sensuality and elegance aroused in them. Diego Dolcini was born in Naples, Italy, and founded his company in 1994. His partnerships with companies like Emilio Pucci, Bulgari, Gucci, Dolce & Gabbana and Max Mara are a testament to his extensive

DIEGO DOLCINI

experience in the industry. Dolcini's shoes represent dreams and emotions, the ideal complement to feminine beauty. Each model is a unique creation, a truly timeless piece with cosmopolitan appeal. His shoes have become true objects of worship, captivating stars such as Charlize Theron, Nicole Kidman, Julia Roberts, Mariah Carey, Jennifer Lopez, Sophie Marceau, Salma Hayek and Monica Bellucci, among others. Elegance, femininity and luxury are signature characteristics of Diego Dolcini shoes.

*Elegance, femininity and luxury
are signature characteristics of
Diego Dolcini shoes.*

Satin and calfskin sandal with gold trim and metallic heel (Fall-Winter 2010-2011).

Satin and kangaroo leather
ankle boot with metallic heel
(Fall-Winter 2010-2011).

Satin court shoe with Swarovski crystal-studded heel. Made exclusively for use in *Addiction*, the short film that premiered in 2012 at the film and fashion festival A Shaded View on Fashion Film (ASVOFF).

  Flat calfskin sandal. Exhibited for the first time at the Limited/Unlimited fashion exhibition in Rome in 2011.

Laminated leather stiletto court shoe
(Fall-Winter 2009-2010).

  Calfskin sandal with laminated leather origami-style trim (Fall-Winter 2009-2010).

Multicolored calfskin and satin
sandal with Swarovski crystal trim
(Spring-Summer 2012).

Multicolored calfskin and satin sandal with wedge heel encrusted with Swarovski crystals (Spring-Summer 2012).

Multicolored python,
leather and satin sandal
(Fall-Winter 2010-2011).

Flat multicolored leather sandal with metallic trim (Spring-Summer 2012).

Pink suede boot
(Fall-Winter 2010-2011).

Calfskin sandal with
multiple metallic circles
(Fall-Winter 2010-2011).

Satin court shoe with Swarovski crystal trim. Made exclusively for use in *Addiction*, the short film that premiered in 2012 at the film and fashion festival A Shaded View on Fashion Film (ASVOFF).

Satin sandal with organdy and handmade Swarovski crystal trim. Exhibited for the first time at the Limited/Unlimited fashion exhibition in Rome in 2010.

Black leather and suede ankle boot
(Fall-Winter 2011-2012).

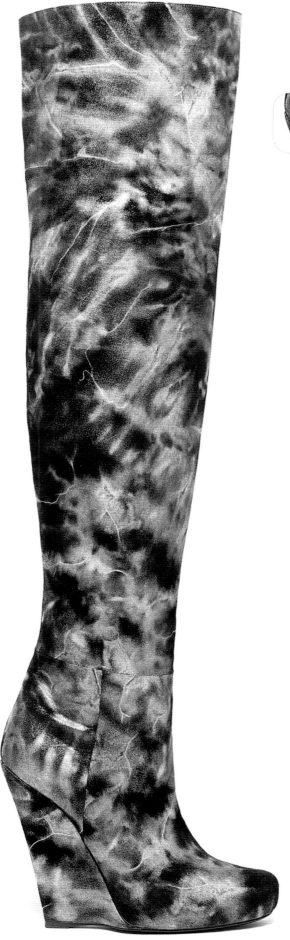

Leather wedge boot
(Fall-Winter 2010-2011).

Ellen Verbeek's shoe collection is the result of her emphasis on meticulous selection of materials, quality craftsmanship and innovative design. Her shoes are manufactured in Italy by expert artisans devoted to the high-quality guarantee of their products. After creating prototypes of each model and performing extensive tests, additional improvements and adjustments are made before embarking on the manufacturing process. Playful, femi-

ELLEN VERBEEK

nine designs characterize each of her collections, along with a scrupulous choice of materials to ensure durability and easy care. Furthermore, the vegetable tanned leather she uses contains no chromium, so her shoes are environmentally friendly and do not cause allergic reactions. In short, Ellen Verbeek's collections feature exclusive, high-quality shoes thanks to her original designs and her clear preference for lasting materials.

Ellen Verbeek's shoes feature scrupulously selected materials to ensure durability and quality.

Black and orange chamois court shoe
with concealed leather platform,
rounded toe and cut-out on the heel
(Fall-Winter 2012-2013).

  Art Deco-style sandal with red and black heel (Summer 2008).

Asymmetrical leather
shoe with inner zip
(Summer 2012).

  Red leather shoe with wooden platform and ankle strap (Summer 2012).

Model inspired by the TV show *Mad Men* with 1950s influences. It can be worn with or without the ankle strap (Summer 2011).

  Black chamois sandal with rubber sole (Summer 2009).

Lacquered red and white
leather high-heeled court shoe
inspired by Art Deco
(Summer 2008).

Black and white court shoe
with wooden heel and rubber
sole inspired by Art Deco
(Fall-Winter 2009-2010).

Aerodynamic-style shoe
inspired by architecture
(Fall-Winter 2009-2010).

Sandal with different colored straps and cut-out wooden wedge heel (Summer 2011).

Cognac color leather sandal
(Summer 2009).

Brown wool-lined shoe
with rounded toe
(Fall-Winter 2009-2010).

White lace-up ankle boot made
of short-haired cowhide
with wooden wedge heel
(Fall-Winter 2010-2011).

Laminated glass, chamois and leather shoe with wooden laser-cut wedge partly covered with leather (Fall-Winter 2012-2013).

Ankle boot with invisible platform
inspired by Art Deco
(Fall-Winter 2008-2009).

Ankle boot made of natural
materials inspired by the 1950s
(Summer 2011).

What exactly is a comfortable shoe? How should it feel when you wear it regularly as part of your daily routine? To the Spanish company Gadea, a comfortable shoe should be light, with a sense of weightlessness, so that with each step you are oblivious to the fact that you are actually wearing it. Gadea shoes are manufactured entirely in Spain at the hands of master shoe crafters, who give shape to patterns, molds and leathers with the confidence conferred by their passion and many years of experience. Gadea also applies a variety

GADEA

of technical and technological improvements during the manufacturing process that enable it to guarantee all of its designs can be worn comfortably. Gadea strives to create a product that will help to make a woman feel strong and confident while she's wearing them. Sometimes words are not enough to describe the different emotions that people feel day to day and the experiences that they take with them. Gadea's goal is to create shoes that can be used as a way for people to express their emotions and experiences.

*Gadea shoes are characterized
by a sense of lightness and
weightlessness.*

Red suede sandal with leather
flower trim and wooden heel
(Spring-Summer 2012).

Peep toe sandal in red
suede with low heel
(Spring-Summer 2012).

High pink espadrille wedge sandal with mocha-colored leather trim (Spring-Summer 2012).

  Beige suede sandal with jute wedge and flower trim (Spring-Summer 2012).

Grass green patent leather
sandal with cork wedge heel
(Spring-Summer 2012).

Multicolored suede sandal
with jute and suede wedge heel
(Spring-Summer 2012).

Mocha-colored textured leather
sandal with concealed platform
and stacked wooden heel
(Spring-Summer 2012).

Green suede sandal
with concealed platform
(Spring-Summer 2012).

Snakeskin print leather court shoe in gray tones with stacked block heel (Fall-Winter 2012-2013).

Black pony skin court shoe
with stacked block heel
(Fall-Winter 2012-2013).

Country style olive suede ankle boot with mocha-colored leather buckles (Fall-Winter 2012-2013).

   Multicolored Oxford style
suede shoe with rubber sole
(Fall-Winter 2012-2013).

Oxford style gray suede ankle boot
with covered wedge and suede trim
(Fall-Winter 2012-2013).

Khaki patent leather ankle boot
with inner zip, fold-down top
and rubber sole and heel
(Fall-Winter 2012-2013).

Oil tanned burgundy suede boot
with high heel and platform
(Fall-Winter 2012-2013).

High-heeled brown brushed leather boot with rubber sole and heel and inner zip (Fall-Winter 2012-2013).

The Italian firm Geox, famous for its philosophy on comfortable shoes, interprets the feminine universe with ergonomic, soft, flexible designs at the service of elegance. Their footwear features patented technological innovations created to make women's shoes more comfortable, and the company is well known for its blend of comfort and elegance. This blend is achieved with Geox's patented perforated rubber soles that contain a special membrane whose microscopic structure maintains the ideal microclimate inside

GEOX

the shoe. This ensures that sweat can be absorbed and expelled while repelling water from outside the shoe at the same time. With its patented leather, Geox unites waterproof properties with the natural breathability of leather soles. The firm has unquestionably found the perfect balance between comfort and style in each of its creations. Their shoes are created for women who are in charge of their own lives and who are proud of their femininity.

Geox has successfully blended the concepts of comfort and design.

Ivana

Brown leather strappy sandal
with heel and platform
(Spring-Summer 2012).

Ivana

Red leather sandal with knotted scarf at the ankle (Spring-Summer 2012).

Ivana

White and turquoise sandal
with high heel and platform
(Spring-Summer 2012).

Janira
Three-toned platform sandal
with zip closure on the instep
(Spring-Summer 2012).

Peonia
Brown wedge sandal
with trim and ankle strap
(Spring-Summer 2012).

Egizia
Two-toned sandal with
ankle and instep straps
(Spring-Summer 2012).

Ella

Camel-colored suede shoe
with high heel and zip trim
(Fall-Winter 2012).

Off-white shoe with low heel
(Spring-Summer 2012).

Ayana
Red suede boot with platform
and mountaineer-style closure
(Fall-Winter 2012).

Armonia

Red moccasin with
wedge heel and tassel trim
(Fall-Winter 2012).

Comfort, design, color and quality are the words that best summarize the spirit of Grotesque. This Dutch footwear brand, founded in 2006 by designer, entrepreneur and photographer Geert Slaats, is known for its use of organically treated top Italian leathers. It is also famous for creating its shoes exclusively in artisan workshops across Europe. In fact, each of its shoes is handmade with consummate passion. The company's designs tend to draw attention with their particular mix of elegance and

GROTESQUE

casualness and vintage aesthetic. Each of its models conceals a surprising detail in color, material and texture, conveying values such as quality, design and exclusivity. The brand has presence in the most exclusive shops in fashion capitals including London, Paris, New York and Barcelona. The Grotesque style continues its relentless growth, inundating cities such as Tokyo, Tel Aviv, Copenhagen, Berlin, Amsterdam, Los Angeles....

*Quality, textures
and colors are
among Grotesque's
strong points.*

Selene Clog

Clog-sandal paying tribute
to the creator's Dutch roots
(Spring-Summer 2010).

Athena Bootie
Leather ankle boot
(Spring-Summer 2011).

La Vie Biker Belt
Brown boot with buckles
(Fall-Winter 2012).

La Vie en Rose

Brown lace-up ankle boot
with high heel
(Fall-Winter 2012).

Dutchess
Urban rock-style leather boot
(Fall-Winter 2012).

La Lune
Casual leather boot
(Fall-Winter 2010).

Deux Chevaux
Equestrian-inspired tall boot
(Fall-Winter 2010).

Princess Knee Boot
Urban rock-style tall boot
(Fall-Winter 2012).

Normandy-born French designer Guillaume Hinfray forged his career in Paris working for haute couture firms such as Nina Ricci, Rochas, Lanvin and Hermès. In the early 1990s, Hinfray left the French capital to quench his thirst for new adventures, embarking upon a new stage of his career in Milan, where he studied new trends alongside Marco Censi. In 2002, Hinfray launched his own line of women's shoes. Since then, "season after season I seek inspiration from my forays through the history of Normandy and my Viking ancestors," claims the designer. His style is a crucible of

GUILLAUME HINFRAY

Mediterranean cultures based on contrasts—an aesthetic collage that harks back to his roots. Many of his designs exude a highly feminine charm with a masculine note, and they entail a journey into the past, especially the Middle Ages. The brand's goal is to offer high-end footwear with an alternative, contemporary vision. Thanks to his elegant style, which combines premium materials with rustic finishes and refined details, Guillaume Hinfray brings a touch of culture and passion to the creation of each of his works.

*The company style,
based on contrasts,
is a crucible of
Mediterranean cultures
inspired by Guillaume
Hinfray's ancestors.*

Scalio

Green suede court shoe with high heel (Spring-Summer 2009).

Hermin
Shoe inspired by the Middle Ages, with embossing and floral motifs in a blend of leather, silk and satin (Fall-Winter 2005-2006).

Jardin

Off-white court shoe with high
heel and satin bow at the toe
(Spring-Summer 2005).

Perle
High-heeled sandal with
metallic bead trim at the vamp
(Fall-Winter 2010-2011).

Modi

Black high-heeled court shoe with heel trim emulating a piercing, one of the firm's signature features (Fall-Winter 2007-2008).

Sainte Trinité
Black court shoe with high heel inspired by the Gothic cathedrals of Normandy, the designer's birthplace (Spring-Summer 2004).

Haris
Black lambskin shoe
(Fall-Winter 2008-2009).

Moon
High-heeled shoe with metallic trim on the heel and toe (Fall-Winter 2008-2009).

Colombelles

Wedge sandal with wooden pattern mimicking the half-timbered walls of the homes in Normandy (Spring-Summer 2010).

Mathilde
Wedge ankle strap sandal with gold trim reminiscent of barbarian jewels (Fall-Winter 2005-2006).

Bobine

Ankle boot with peep toe and leather straps that wrap the foot for a "mummy" effect (Spring-Summer 2012).

Cambrioleuse
Three-toned ankle boot
with metal staple trim
(Fall-Winter 2012-2013).

Dimenche
Brown leather and suede ankle boot
(Fall-Winter 2011-2012).

Bomlo
Two-toned leather ankle boot featuring a design reminiscent of a tattoo (Fall-Winter 2009-2010).

Asi
Lace-up classic cut masculine shoe
(pre-Fall 2009).

Osmose

Black shoe draped
with transparent mesh
(Spring-Summer 2012).

"Intropia" is a combination of the words "interior" and "utopia," meaning a utopia that is born inside of a woman, who then projects it to the outside world through her interests, experiences and dreams realized. This idea is clearly what the Spanish brand Hoss aims to project with every design. Created in Madrid in 1994, this fashion and accessories brand strives to offer original, feminine and inspiring shoes. Contemporary, varied, eclectic and cosmopolitan are some of the adjectives that could describe the Hoss Intropia style.

HOSS INTROPIA

The use of a variety of materials and fastidious design are also part of the company's ethos. Each of its collections arises from numerous sources of inspiration, and they are designed so that a variety of unique women can find a way to reflect their personalities. In fact, the company's philosophy is that fashion's main purpose is to help each woman be herself, a real challenge that Hoss Intropia rises to with style and panache.

Contemporary, varied, eclectic and cosmopolitan are some of the adjectives that could describe the Hoss Intropia style.

Aged gold-effect sandal with embroidered ribbon trim (Fall-Winter 2012-2013).

Aged gold-effect sandal
with ankle strap
(Fall-Winter 2012-2013).

Sandal with a blend of
different leathers and a
wraparound ankle strap
(Spring-Summer 2012).

Pale pink patent leather sandal with ankle strap and wooden sole and heel (Spring-Summer 2012).

Suede sandal in
multiple powdery shades
(Fall-Winter 2012-2013).

Leather and sackcloth shoe
(Spring-Summer 2012).

Painted raffia court shoe
(Spring-Summer 2011).

  Camel leather and black
patent leather gladiator sandal
(Spring-Summer 2012).

Dark red velvet wedge sandal
(Fall-Winter 2011-2012).

Mary Jane dark red leather sandal
(Fall-Winter 2010-2011).

Painted raffia sandal
(Spring-Summer 2011).

Blue suede animal print court shoe
(Fall-Winter 2012-2013).

Peep toe black lace ankle boot
(Fall-Winter 2012-2013).

  Metallic leather flat ankle boot
(Fall-Winter 2012-2013).

Suede wedge clog
(Spring-Summer 2012).

Flat gray fur boot
(Fall-Winter 2011-2012).

Iris Morata is a Spanish brand that was founded in Barcelona in 2006 as an expression of the yearning of its designer, Iris Morata, to create a different kind of shoe. Her drive and entrepreneurial spirit led her to create her own brand before she had finished her degree in fashion and footwear design. The first collection, La Impaciencia (Impatience), reflected one of its restless young designer's most prominent personality traits. That summer collection was bold and brimming with color, featuring

IRIS MORATA

flats and medium height shoes along with sandal-boots that possessed a somewhat innocent air. Without losing the momentum of that collection, the brand has gradually evolved toward more mature, daring and sophisticated designs: simple, functional, comfortable footwear that are full of charm. Each model is carefully crafted down to the last detail using the best materials and molds, with an emphasis on comfort, design and innovation. Iris Morata provides a unique, high-quality shoe with character targeted at today's woman and her youthful, feminine, risk-embracing spirit.

The company philosophy is to seek perfection in both craftsmanship and design.

Two-toned court shoe with interlinked motif on the outside. Concealed platform and bamboo-covered heel (Fall-Winter 2009-2010).

Low multicolored ankle boot in earth tones. Double platform and bamboo-covered heel (Fall-Winter 2009-2010).

Court shoe with blue elasticated straps across the instep and bamboo-covered heel (Fall-Winter 2009-2010).

Stingray-effect leather court shoe with elasticated straps across the instep, covered heel and double platform (Fall-Winter 2009-2010).

Snakeskin-embossed
turquoise leather sandal
(Spring-Summer 2009).

Multicolored sandal with ankle strap and buckle, concealed platform and wooden heel (Spring-Summer 2009).

Red suede sandal with T-strap
(Fall-Winter 2011-2012).

  Red suede ankle boot with black elastic inserts on the sides (Fall-Winter 2011-2012).

Red ankle boot with two textures: matte on the foot and shiny on the fold-down cuff (Fall-Winter 2008-2009).

Red ankle boot with leopard print toe, back seam covering and trim (Fall-Winter 2008-2009).

Silver medium-heeled ankle boot
(Fall-Winter 2007-2008).

Sage green ankle boot with fringe at the ankle. Model with an inner zip, bamboo-covered heel and concealed platform (Fall-Winter 2009-2010).

Tall boot in two textures of gray: shiny and matte. Knotted plaited trim on the upper and rubber heel (Fall-Winter 2009-2010).

Flat boot with wide upper. Lower part in stingray-effect leather and natural matte leather upper (Fall-Winter 2008-2009).

Camel-colored wedge boot
lined with rabbit fur.
Strap with adjustable buckle
(Fall-Winter 2007-2008).

Camel-colored over the knee
boot with perforated trim
and wooden heel
(Fall-Winter 2007-2008).

Since its inception in 2000, the California-based Jeffrey Campbell has found inspiration for his designs in a variety of places: from vintage style, haute couture catwalks and modern women. Founded as a small, family-owned company, its meteoric rise started with a true passion for design. Despite becoming a global brand with headquarters in Los Angeles, Jeffrey Campbell retains the family-oriented ideals and principles upon which the company was founded, and its entrepreneurial spirit

JEFFREY CAMPBELL

continues to be found in the way the company develops its designs. Jeffrey Campbell constantly seeks new sources of inspiration, concepts and details that, when combined, can create the different styles that the firm showcases season after season. Its '70s style is ideal for creating hippie and rock and roll looks, and its most famous models (like the iconic Lita) come in such a wide variety of color and fabric combinations that it is difficult to choose a favorite. Jeffrey Campbell's bold designs are winning fans all over the world.

Jeffrey Campbell draws inspiration from vintage style, contemporary trends and everyday life.

Skate
White ankle boot with
carved wooden wedge heel
(Spring 2011).

Tick Wash
Pink suede ankle boot
(Spring-Summer 2011).

Tie
Gold glitter-encrusted ankle boot
(Winter 2010).

So Crazy

Leather court shoe with gold
hologram and Mary Jane ankle strap
(Spring 2011).

 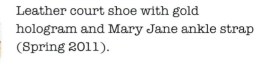

Daisy D
Leopard print sandal with ankle strap
(Spring 2010).

Big Girl Purple Combo
Platform sandal with
wooden heel and stripe print
(Spring 2011).

Everest
Brown leather model
(Spring 2011).

Lita

Navy blue suede model.
The Lita model is Jeffrey
Campbell's most famous creation,
available in hundreds of prints,
fabrics and leathers
(Spring 2010).

Zip 2
Black wedge with multiple buckles (Spring 2011).

Mary Roks
Black suede peep toe
wedge with side cut-outs
(Spring 2009).

Canadian designer Jerome C. Rousseau's shoes are true objects of seduction, and each of his collections oozes elegance, style and femininity. His interest in design was shaped through art and music: "I started drawing shoes as a teenager after watching a Deee-Lite video clip. I was influenced by its unique styling, but it was the overstated retro footwear that first caught my attention," the designer explains. Jerome C. Rousseau launched the brand bearing his name with his Fall 2008 collection. After gaining a great deal of technical shoe design knowledge at London's Cordwainers College, he

JEROME C. ROUSSEAU

had the opportunity to spend ten years fine-tuning his skills as a designer in London and Los Angeles, where he worked with Matthew Williamson, Isabella Fiore, John Richmond and John Rocha. The designer firmly believes that a pair of shoes can transform a woman's personality, attitude, character and movement as she walks. "I initially thought in terms of shape, silhouette and structure when I was designing. Later I started to bring fashion into the equation," he notes. Modern art, European design, pop culture and nightlife are just some of Jerome C. Rousseau's sources of inspiration.

Modern art, European design, pop culture and nightlife are just some of Jerome C. Rousseau's sources of inspiration.

Medusa
Multicolored strappy sandal
(Spring 2009).

Aizza
Green glitter court shoe.
This model has appeared every
season since Fall-Winter 2009
(Spring 2010).

Dragon
Multicolored suede court shoe with gold trim from Jerome C. Rousseau's first collection (Fall-Winter 2008).

Ysy.
Multicolored suede sandal
(Fall-Winter 2011).

Elli
Leather peep toe ankle boot
(Spring 2012).

Elli
Leather peep toe ankle boot
(Spring 2012).

Quorra

Futuristic silver leather sandal
made in partnership with Disney.
This design, inspired by the
1982 film *Tron*, commemorates
the 2010 sequel, *Tron: Legacy*
(Spring 2011).

Antinea
Metallic leather Art Deco
peep toe court shoe
(Fall-Winter 2010).

Kio Loops

Black suede peep toe court shoe
with platinum leather trim
(Spring 2012).

Kier
Black satin peep toe d'Orsay court shoe with bows at the toe and gold leather trim (Fall-Winter 2012).

Hoc
Animal print ankle boot
(Fall-Winter 2012).

Nares
Orange embossed ostrich peep toe ankle boot with side cut-out (Spring 2012).

Riviera
Suede peep toe ankle boot
(Fall-Winter 2012).

Lenka
Fuchsia suede peep toe platform court shoe (Fall-Winter 2011).

Artemis
Blue denim-toned leather ankle boot
(Fall-Winter 2010).

Comet Tassel

Black leather peep toe with tassel trim (Fall-Winter 2010).

The couple behind this Icelandic brand are Hugrún Árnadóttir and Magni Thorsteinsson. These two creative forces have a strong aesthetic vision and are united by their love of color and the creative process. Kron by KronKron was founded in 2008, the year the company unveiled its first shoe collection. Thanks to its success, they added a clothing line in 2010. Each of their collections is colorful, original and detailed. The designs, which are crafted in the Spanish town of Elda, are not limited to each season's trends since the

KRON BY KRONKRON

Kron by KronKron spirit is timeless. Their footwear line reflects a youthful, fun style with a mix of textures and colors in each shoe, rendering each piece unique and highly personal. Their designs include everything from court shoes and lace-ups to ankle boots, all with a colorful touch and a carefully designed informal style. They are unquestionably ebullient shoes that demand to be noticed, ideal for women who want to stand out with every step they take.

*Kron by KronKron's
designs are colorful,
timeless and feminine.*

Court shoe with padded
sides and high heel
(Spring-Summer 2011).

High-heeled suede court shoe
(Spring-Summer 2011).

Court shoe with
high heel and frill trim
(Fall-Winter 2011-2012).

Multicolored high-heeled court shoe with frills and stitching (Spring-Summer 2012).

High-heeled court shoe
with trim on the arch
(Spring-Summer 2010).

Multicolored court shoe
with high heel and frill trim
(Fall-Winter 2012-2013).

High-heeled leather court shoe
(Fall-Winter 2012-2013).

High-heeled suede court shoe
(Spring-Summer 2011).

Court shoe with low heel
(Spring-Summer 2010).

  Court shoe with low heel
and suede flower trim
(Spring-Summer 2011).

High-heeled shoe with button trim
(Fall-Winter 2011-2012).

Lace-up platform shoe
(Fall-Winter 2010-2011).

Three-toned suede ankle boot
(Fall-Winter 2010-2011).

Suede lace-up ankle boot
(Fall-Winter 2010-2011).

Lace-up ankle boot
(Fall-Winter 2010-2011).

Zip front ankle boot
(Fall-Winter 2012-2013).

Lodi was founded in 1978 in Elda, in the Spanish province of Alicante. Over the years, it has grown to become an international footwear company with products available in over 30 countries and clients on three continents. The secret of each pair of Lodi shoes lies in the hands of every single person who takes part in their manufacture. Expert hands give shape to the leather in a living process that begins on the drafting table and ends with the finished boxed shoe. Each season the Lodi design team creates 500 new models, but only a chosen few end up join-

ing the collection. This thoughtful process is key because each decision is weighed according to the trends in a particular season. Once the collection is selected, the manufacturing process gets underway, during which each shoe may pass through up to 80 different hands before being finished. This process involves complex choreography and almost everything is crafted by hand with only the simplest jobs automated. The process begins with the fastidious selection of materials and meticulous design.

Lodi is synonymous with quality and expert craftmanship wrought with care and love, with hours spent merging trends, fashion and the real world for real women.

Orange suede ballet flat
with bow on the toe
(Spring-Summer 2012).

  Blue suede ballet flat
with pom-pom on the toe
(Fall-Winter 2011-2012).

Peep toe sandal with high heel
and platform covered in fuchsia
suede with leather trim
(Spring-Summer 2010).

Brightly colored punched sandal with skinny straps (Spring-Summer 2009).

Snakeskin embossed court shoe
with ankle and heel strap in a
brilliant green with gold trim
(Fall-Winter 2012-2013).

  Nude patent leather
sandal with high heel
(Spring-Summer 2012).

Sandal with metallic suede
straps and black back zip
(Spring-Summer 2011).

Skinny-strapped sandal with back zip
(Spring-Summer 2011).

Blue and brown court shoe with
platform and high block heel
(Fall-Winter 2012-2013).

High-heeled platform sandal in a combination of blue suede and embossed leather (Spring-Summer 2012).

Oxford-style shoe-boot
in brushed white
(Spring-Summer 2008).

Beige Oxford-style shoe with patent leather cut-outs (Spring-Summer 2008).

Camel-colored suede
Oxford-style shoe
(Spring-Summer 2009).

Patchwork shoe-boot of reptile-effect embossed leather in brown tones (Fall-Winter 2009-2010).

Lace-up mocha-colored
boot with elasticated wool
(Fall-Winter 2008-2009).

Brown embossed patent
leather boot with flat heel
(Fall-Winter 2008-2009).

Marc Jacobs is probably the most famous and unpredictable of all the American designers. He is the designer with the most Council of Fashion Designers of America (CFDA) award nominations and wins, he is also the youngest designer to win the CFDA's prestigious Perry Ellis Award for New Fashion Talent. He has been nicknamed the King Midas of Fashion by many fans since he and his partner Robert Duffy designed their first collection under the Marc Jacobs label back in 1986. This New Yorker,

MARC JACOBS

who has a fascination with Paris, mixes couture inspiration with elements of urban culture and ethnic design—inspired by the New York metropolitan lifestyle. His designs are perennially provocative, groundbreaking and trendy. His unique creations encompass all styles imaginable, oozing fashion thanks to their impeccable details and unpredictable evocations. Likewise, his role as artistic director for Louis Vuitton gives him a special vantage point for determining and predicting what will be worn each season.

Marc Jacobs shoes reflect the atmosphere of New York and are evidence of his admirable trendsetting skills.

Burgundy-colored high-heeled sandal with ankle buckle.

  Two-toned sandal tied at the ankle with tassel trim.

Multicolored sandal
with ankle strap.

Blue and gold shoe with tassel trim.

Lace-up masculine gold shoe.

Gold shoe with gemstone buckle.

Turquoise court shoe with high heel.

High-heeled sandal in blues with
beaded trim and ankle strap.

Ankle tie sandal with tassel trim and multicolored hearts.

Black sandal trimmed with tiny multicolored bows.

Two-toned black and fuchsia sandal
with ankle strap.

Sandal trimmed
with colored circles.

Sandal trimmed
with colored circles.

Multicolored high-heeled sandal.

Strappy high-heeled sandal
with bow trim at the toe.

Strappy black sandal
with gold high heel and sole.

Founded in 1971, the Brazilian company Melissa creates authentic works of pop art that stand out for their exclusive injected thermoplastic technology. With its modern shapes and organic lines, Melissa footwear clearly heralds plastic as its star material because it is malleable, flexible, comfortable and soft. The company has played a significant role in this material's transformation into a symbol of glamor. It tasks itself with finding state-of-the-art technology to use in conjunction with innovative shapes,

MELISSA

colors and finishes. Throughout its history, Melissa has based its ideology on three principles that are clearly captured in each of its creations: innovation, creativity and irreverence. Likewise, the originality and functionality of its designs stem from the use of bright colors, attractive shapes and beautiful finishes. With these key elements, Melissa strives to create unusual yet feminine shoes for daring women who want to define their style by their footwear. This challenge is one that Melissa rises to day after day.

Melissa focuses on creations that have style, irreverence and boldness, using plastic as its star material.

Amazonas

High-heeled sandal with a band across the vamp inspired by the colors, shapes and grandeur of Amazonian culture (Spring-Summer 2011).

Patchuli

Beige platform sandal with ankle
strap. The platform has a band of
color along the entire sole, inspired
by the latex of rubber trees
(Spring-Summer 2011).

Melissa + Gaetano Pesce
Transparent ankle boot with
interconnecting circles made of
flexible, elastic materials
by Melissa + Gaetano Pesce
(Spring-Summer 2011).

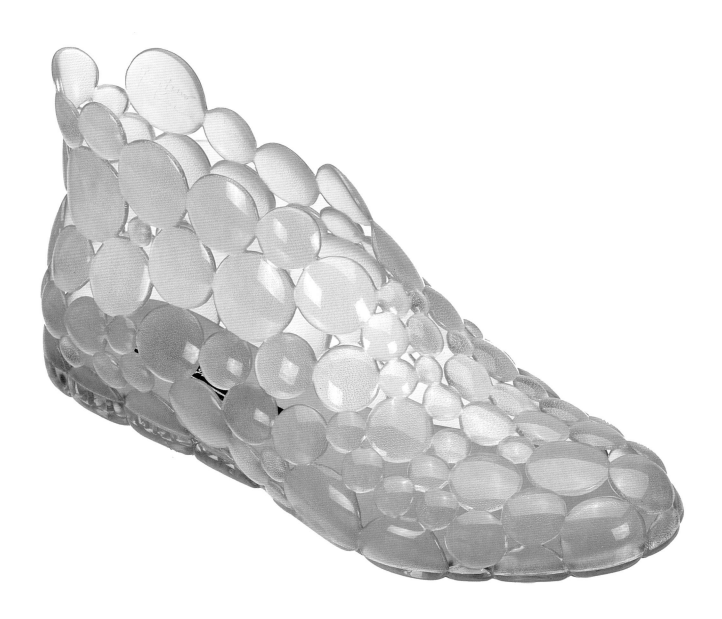

Liberty
Gladiator sandal with ankle strap
(Spring-Summer 2011).

Campana Papel

Ballet flat reminiscent of the shapes and textures of cardboard boxes by Irmãos Campana + Melissa (Spring-Summer 2012).

Melissa Ultragirl + J. Maskrey
Pink ballet flat sprinkled with tiny
crystals by Melissa + J. Maskrey
(Spring-Summer 2008).

Croco

Burgundy Mary Jane with fake reptile print and heart-shaped buckle by Vivienne Westwood Anglomania + Melissa (Fall-Winter 2008).

Incense

Court shoe with high heel and heel trim inspired by the 1950s (Fall-Winter 2012).

Electric

High-heeled gray court
shoe with ankle strap
(Spring-Summer 2012).

Melissa + Jean Paul Gaultier
Plastic high-heeled sandal with
opaque and transparent straps
by Melissa + Jean Paul Gaultier
(Fall-Winter 2010).

Scarfun

Fuchsia court shoe with pointed toe by Alexandre Herchcovitch + Melissa (Spring-Summer 2007).

Melissa + Karim Rashid
Gold plastic drop-shaped court
shoe by Melissa + Karim Rashid
(Fall-Winter 2009).

Aileron
Two-toned gladiator shoe
by Gareth Pugh + Melissa
(Spring-Summer 2012).

Melissa n° 1
High-heeled sandal with ankle strap
by Pedro Lourenço + Melissa
(Spring-Summer 2013).

Melissa Ultragirl

Flat shoe with tiny peep toe created from Melflex, a particularly strong, flexible and soft material (Fall-Winter 2005).

Divine
Black and fuchsia ballet flat
with bow trim on the toe
by Pedro Lourenço + Melissa
(Spring-Summer 2013).

Paco Gil doesn't just create shoes, he creates art for the feet. The key lies in their impeccable shape and meticulous design, as well as in his use of premium materials. Paco Gil's Spanish headquarters are in Elda, Alicante and were founded in 1982 by Paco Gil, Juan Carlos Gil and Rafael Gómez. The designer is entirely self-taught: learning from his professional experience in the sector, his constant travels and his deep-seated admiration of women with character, the kind who leave their mark as

PACO GIL

they walk through life. Each of his designs is an absolute treat featuring well-defined lines and geometric shapes elevated to the utmost by their sky-high heels, fine materials and by the artisan hands that craft each one as if it were a sculpture. Thanks to his innovative, sophisticated designs, his collections are trendsetters and clear points of reference for all women who believe that shoes are an essential accessory for any wardrobe.

Paco Gil's shoes are a treat for the feet, with well-defined lines and geometric shapes elevated to the utmost by their sky-high heels.

Galerna

Sandal-boot with a curved maxi-wedge in a mix of fuchsia leathers with contrasting white platform and matching laces (Spring-Summer 2012).

Lebeche
Coral red suede court shoe
with matching patent leather
platform and curved heel
(Spring-Summer 2012).

Velour

Brown split-leather maxi-wedge sandal with pastel green platform, off-white elastic strap on the instep and side closure with tiny silver buckle (Spring-Summer 2012).

Strappy sandal with maxi heel
and off-white platform
(Spring-Summer 2009).

Bombón

Multicolored court shoe
with concealed platform
and patches of cinnamon,
chocolate and cognac suede
(Fall-Winter 2011-2012).

Columbia

Court shoe with wide gathered vamp
and babydoll heel in burgundy suede.
Flower needlepoint trim in green
tones to the back
(Fall-Winter 2012-2013).

Land

Light brown sandal with suede double platform, maxi heel, brown Sioux-style straps and gold buckles (Spring-Summer 2010).

High-heeled camel suede sandal
with aged gold leather straps
and natural platform sole
(Spring-Summer 2012).

Licorice

Black split-leather sandal
with contrasting off-white ribbon
stitching and tassels, high-heeled
and concealed platform
(Spring-Summer 2011).

Poivre

Denver black sandal-boot with natural hemp elastic bands across the vamp and decorative steel rivets (Spring-Summer 2011).

Loafer-cut court shoe with oversized
Dalmatian print ponyskin upper,
curved platform and heel covered
in black patent leather
(Fall-Winter 2012-2013).

Amaretto

Peep toe shoe-boot in leopard
print ponyskin, with V-shaped vamp
and deep red patent leather trim
(Fall-Winter 2011-2012).

Tatty

Blue suede ankle boot with a rounded toe and loose, scrunched upper. Curved burgundy suede platform and maxi heel (Fall-Winter 2012-2013).

Green suede ankle boot with slashed toe, architectural heel and side cut-out secured with strap (Fall-Winter 2012-2013).

Called by many the new *bottier* of the 21st century, the young Almerian-born Patricia Rosales has successfully defined her own style with each design. Her models, known as "Patricias" by celebrities, are veritable gems; her footwear has been elevated to the status of fine jewellery in her *prêt-à-porter* collections. Her fascination with shoes began at an early age, when she began to collect them solely based on what they conveyed to her. Over the years, she has developed an ethos based on designing footwear for women who define their look from the feet up. Each shoe,

PATRICIA ROSALES

with its trademark pearl on the heel curve, is a sumptuous work of art featuring the most exquisite materials, including napped crocodile skin, eel skin, stingray leather, emu feathers, python, mink with satin, suede, patent leather, blue sapphires, black diamonds, emeralds and cultivated pearls. To the designer's mind, the "soul" of a shoe is what makes each of these beautiful objects special, unique and outstanding. This uniqueness may lie in an isolated detail, a fine material, a gemstone, or the shoe as a whole.

Patricia Rosales firmly believes in "shoes with a soul," shoes in a league of their own.

Katya
Red velvet beaded shoe
with gold maxi platform
(Fall-Winter 2011-2012).

Éveline

Leather turquoise satin ankle boot set with topaz, citrine, pink tourmaline, amethyst, moonstone and peridot (Spring-Summer 2012).

Paillardise

Turquoise satin shoe with spider web and diamond, emerald and sapphire brooch (Spring-Summer 2012).

Alla
Satin and rhinestone court shoe
(Fall-Winter 2011-2012).

Pudeur

Laminated leather shoe with
fine jewel trim in gold with
multicolored sapphires,
citrines and burnt ostrich feathers.

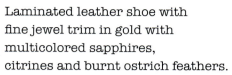

Carrousel
Embossed high-heeled shoe
(Fall-Winter 2011-2012).

Halcón
Black leather sandal
with gold falcon trim
(Spring-Summer 2011).

Theatre
Black shoe
(Fall-Winter 2011-2012).

Elena
Black high-heeled shoe
with feathers at the toe
(Fall-Winter 2011-2012).

Alexander

Black suede and mink ankle boot with baroque buttons (Fall-Winter 2011-2012).

Yulia
Three-toned ankle boot
with rhinestone trim
(Fall-Winter 2011-2012).

The Spanish company Pons Quintana was founded by Santiago Pons Quintana in 1953 in Alaior, Minorca. The current generation at the helm of the business includes his children Magdalena and Santiago Pons-Quintana Palliser. The firm's trademark plaiting was first used in fashion footwear in the late 1960s, heralding a unique, unmistakable style. The traditional plait, which is now highly technically evolved, keeps the culture of craftsmanship alive, merging past and present through design. The sewing of the shoes,

PONS QUINTANA

the assembly of each piece, leather finishing and polishing, packaging and distribution are all done in Minorca using a production system that blends manual labor and automation. A tiny portion of the plaiting and cutting process is outsourced to other countries. Once the pieces have been sewn, they go through a series of phases that range from sole and heel assembly (gluing and stapling) to leather polishing, preparing the finishes (matte, shiny, worn, etc.) and the impeccable quality control that is the hallmark of this brand.

Pons Quintana's plaited shoes have become one of the company's trademarks.

Lemon yellow wedge sandal with
thin plaited straps and rubber sole
(Summer 2009).

  Coral-colored narrow plaited court shoe with leather-covered heel (Summer 2011).

Metallic plaited ballet flat
with trim at the toe
(Summer 2012).

Multicolored plaited ballet
flat with leather sole
(Summer 2011).

Wedge sandal with plaited color
block straps and rubber sole
(Summer 2011).

  Fuchsia plaited sandal
with leather-covered heel
(Summer 2011).

Plaited metallic sandal
with leather-covered wedge heel
(Summer 2011).

Plaited sandal with leather tassels, ankle strap and leather-covered heel (Summer 2010).

Jewel-encrusted python print
sandal with ankle strap, cork
platform and metallic leather
(Summer 2012).

  Plaited multistrap sandal in metallic tones with cork-covered platform (Summer 2012).

Two-toned plaited sandal
with cork-covered platform
(Summer 2012).

Sandal with thin plaited black straps and heel covered in python print leather (Summer 2010).

Gray suede ankle boot with folds on the side and Bottier-style heel (Fall-Winter 2012-2013).

  Black plaited ankle boot with leather sole and heel (Fall-Winter 2012-2013).

This iconic Italian company was founded in 1913 by Mario Prada, and his granddaughter Miuccia Prada currently reigns one of the most prestigious fashion brands in the world. Its iconic logos, the Savoy coat of arms and the Savoy figure eight knot, reflect the company's history as the official purveyor to the former royal family of Italy. With sophisticated style and enduring quality, the brand's shoes blend craftsmanship and innovation with distinctive originality that represents the best of Italian culture.

PRADA

Prada's ultra-chic, alternative designs reflect the company's working philosophy. Attention to detail, quality materials and innovative manufacturing techniques have helped this celebrated brand become one of the major pioneers of luxury fashion and industry trends. Its steadfast focus on craftsmanship and its fastidious interpretation of design make it one of the top companies in terms of international presence and prestige, and it is surrounded by an aura of exclusivity wherever it goes.

*Prada designs have
sophisticated style and
enduring quality.*

High-heeled reptile leather sandal
(Fall-Winter 2000).

Crocodile shoe with wedge heel
(Spring-Summer 2006).

Black and blue patent leather shoe
(Fall-Winter 2008).

Patent leather shoe with fiery trim
(Spring-Summer 2012).

Multicolored python leather shoe
(Spring-Summer 2009).

Multicolored plaited leather
shoe handmade in India
(Spring-Summer 2011).

Shoe with crystal and plastic drops on the front and heels (Spring-Summer 2010).

Embroidered black satin court shoe
with plastic and metal beading and
Swarovski crystal trim
(Fall-Winter 2009).

Mary Jane court shoe
with embossed floral design
(Fall-Winter 1996).

Patent leather sandal
with elastic ankle band
(Fall-Winter 2007).

Red leather boot with high
heel and rubber sole
(Fall-Winter 2009).

Fuchsia patent leather boot
(Spring-Summer 2006).

Pura López was born and raised in Alicante by a family involved in the shoe industry, so she learned the requisite techniques and know-how from an early age. She furthered her training in interior design, fashion, pattern design and footwear in Spain, New York and Milan. Her collections make her brand a huge contributor to the Spanish fashion industry. In this designer's opinion, a shoe is not merely an accessory but an essential object for expressing femininity and seduction. "In my collections

PURA LÓPEZ

I try to mix fantasy with practicality, eclecticism with vitality. I love playing with colors, shapes and heels until I achieve the perfect balance among all the components of the shoe. But what I enjoy the most is mixing sky-high heels with the finest and subtlest leather strips strategically placed to hold the foot delicately and yet firmly, yielding the sexiest shoe possible," she states. According to Pura López, shoes are a form of communication, revealing the personality of the individual wearing them.

*According to Pura López, shoes
are a form of communication,
revealing the personality of the
individual wearing them.*

Pearl gray satin sandal
(Summer 2009).

Pink satin sandal with ankle bow
(Summer 2010).

Red satin sandal with
cut-out on the vamp
(Fall-Winter 2009).

Red satin peep toe court shoe with back and part of the heel encrusted with crystals (Fall-Winter 2012).

Pink sandal with ankle strap
(Spring-Summer 2011).

Brown raffia sandal with multicolored suede straps (Spring-Summer 2011).

Blue and white strappy
sandal with wooden heel
(Summer 2010).

Navy blue court shoe with wooden sole and heel trimmed with knotted laces (Summer 2010).

Leather ankle boot with rabbit fur and buckles (Winter 2011).

Brown suede ankle boot
with gold wedge
(Fall-Winter 2012).

A master in the art of shoe design, Robert Clergerie has been building on his unique interpretation of shoe creation since 1981. His quest for sobriety, purity, minimalism and simplicity is the driving force behind this French company, whose designs are conspicuous for the originality of their stylistic approach; somewhere between tradition and modernity. The appointment of Roland Mouret as the firm's creative director has ushered in a new era for this brand, and his goal is to incorporate modernity with the Robert Clergerie experience. In his first collection for the brand, Mouret

ROBERT CLERGERIE

has designed his ideal shoe, the kind that never goes out of fashion. To do this, the collection travels back in time to draw inspiration from iconic films and emblematic actresses like Catherine Deneuve in *Belle du Jour*, Faye Dunaway in *The Eyes of Laura Mars* and Michèle Morgan in *Quai des Brumes*. It is a highly cinematographic collection that offers a wide variety of heel heights, architectural volumes and luxurious materials. Featuring a color palette that ranges from earth tones to the deepest greens, the collection is faithful to the aesthetic, spirit and creativity of Robert Clergerie.

The quest for sobriety, purity, minimalism and simplicity is the driving force behind Robert Clergerie's designs.

Drakar
Shiny red sandal with wooden platform and leather heel (Fall-Winter 2012).

Quarto
Classic red suede sandal
(Fall-Winter 2012).

Dorote
Red suede shoe-boot with cut-outs
(Fall-Winter 2012).

Polly
Red suede court shoe
with curved heel
(Fall-Winter 2012).

Larina

Tan leather and brown python
shoe with silver front strap
(Fall-Winter 2012).

Millie
Vintage-style red suede and beige leather sandal (Fall-Winter 2012).

Quaya
Aqua suede shoe with
multiple brown leather straps
(Fall-Winter 2012).

Pia
Gray python court shoe
with green leather trim
(Fall-Winter 2012).

Dillig
Brown leather and pink python
wedge sandal with aqua suede straps
(Fall-Winter 2012).

Delpha
Crocodile and python wedge
sandal in earth tones
(Fall-Winter 2012).

Harum
Sandal with tassel and metal trim inspired by the 1970s (Fall-Winter 2012).

Lorna
Court shoe with three-toned heel and undulating vamp (Fall-Winter 2012).

Talno

Masculine gray leather shoe
with black star-shaped designs
(Fall-Winter 2012).

Quandy
Purple suede Oxford shoe-boot
with curved heel
(Fall-Winter 2012).

Julios
Black patent leather platform boot
(Fall-Winter 2012).

Black leather boot with
trim on the toe and curved heel
(Fall-Winter 2012).

Roberto Cavalli's name is synonymous with glamor, luxury and prestige. Ever since this Italian company was established in the 1970s, its designs have spread all around the world and are regarded as veritable works of art. In the beginning, Cavalli invented and patented a revolutionary method for embossing leather and began to create swatches of various materials. He unveiled these techniques for the first time in Paris and immediately secured commissions from Hermès and Pierre Cardin. The orders from these fashion houses gave him the confidence he needed to start his

ROBERTO CAVALLI

own business. It was an immediate success, and the luxurious textiles, precious leathers, jewel appliqués and flexible leathers soon turned into his trademarks. Roberto Cavalli views fashion as an all-encompassing experience and uses design as a tool to blend personality and sensuality. The style he proposes is not just a way of dressing but a way of being: a lifestyle that blends respect for traditional craftsmanship with a strong yearning to experiment. Roberto Cavalli is unpredictable; his style is constantly evolving in an incessant quest for new technical and artistic solutions.

Roberto Cavalli blends respect for traditional craftsmanship with a strong yearning to experiment.

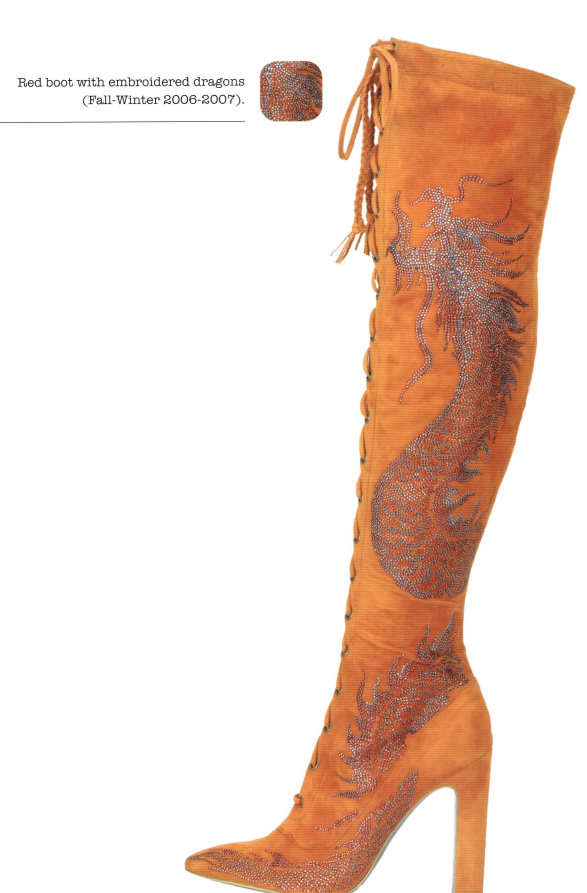

Red boot with embroidered dragons
(Fall-Winter 2006-2007).

Red stiletto with trim at the toe (Spring-Summer 2008).

Stiletto with gem-encrusted serpent
(Spring-Summer 2007).

Stiletto python sandal
(Spring-Summer 2010).

Feline print stiletto
(Fall-Winter 2003-2004).

  Leopard print pony fur court shoe
(Fall-Winter 2009-2010).

Leopard print ankle boot
(Fall-Winter 2012-2013).

Leather boot with buckles
(Fall-Winter 2009-2010).

One hundred years of history have paved the way to Sendra's success. All those years encompass the experience of four generations, from the brand's founder Andrés Sendra to his great-grandson Francisco Javier Sendra, the current director and leader of a team of 170 experts in boot fashion, design and manufacturing. What began as a small family-owned company has become one of the most renowned boot brands in the world thanks to its experience and ability to constantly evolve.

SENDRA

The 250 manufacturing steps of these boots include cutting and shaping the leathers, embroidering or embossing each motif, orchestrating all the elements together and achieving the perfect finish for each boot. However, the most important step is the "Goodyear stitching," which provides the characteristic durability of the brand's boots. Ninety percent of Sendra's boot production is artisanal, making each pair of boots a unique, exclusive item that blends sturdiness, comfort, quality and design in equal measure.

Sendra repeatedly reinvents the cowboy boot, a fashion classic.

Natural cowhide ankle
boot with side zip
(Fall-Winter 2011-2012).

Khaki imitation python
ankle boot with side zip
(Fall-Winter 2011-2012).

Leather ankle boot with
American flag image
(Spring-Summer 2012).

Leather and split-leather
ankle boot with embroidered
triangular Aztec pattern
(Fall-Winter 2011-2012).

Olympia leather boot
with aged gold trim
(Spring-Summer 2012).

Oxide leather boot with fringe on the upper (Fall-Winter 2012-2013).

Taupe leather boot
with riveted eagle design
(Fall-Winter 2009-2010).

Taupe Olympia leather boot
(Spring-Summer 2011).

The young Italian designer Simona Citarella began her professional experience in the footwear industry as the assistant to designer Guillaume Hinfray, and she has worked with avant-garde brands like B Store, Amaterasu, Salvatore Ferragamo, Bottega Veneta, René Lezard and Dolce & Gabbana. Her debut collection was launched under the name Simona Vanth in Spring-Summer 2012. The title of her line, Primitive Plastique, spirits the imagination away to a world where basic materials

SIMONA VANTH

like leather, ceramic, stone and cotton are masterfully manipulated with technically evolved plastics and textures to create ultramodern shapes. To craft the collection, she worked with artist Manon Beuchot, known as Babyscotch, to create a high-end capsule collection and to transform her shoes into true works of art. Every season, Simona Vanth seeks out a contemporary artist with a distinct style to collaborate with in order to bring her projects to fruition. This brand combines the best of Italian luxury workmanship with contemporary design.

Each season, Simona Vanth seeks out a contemporary artist with a distinct style to collaborate with in order to bring her projects to fruition.

Astralopy Nubuck
Flat sandal with knot closure
(Spring-Summer 2012).

Astralopy Miami
Flat sandal with side zip
(Spring-Summer 2012).

Medea Vegetal Calf
Strappy sandal
(Spring-Summer 2012).

Poirot Curl Vegetal Calf
Flat sandal inspired
by Etruscan vases
(Spring-Summer 2012).

Poirot Arielle

Gold ankle boot with chains designed with Canadian jewelry designer Arielle De Pinto (Fall-Winter 2012).

Poirot White Nubuck
White nubuck leather ankle
boot with wedge and peep toe
(Spring-Summer 2012).

Anderson Boot Gold Mirror
Gold leather boot designed
with Canadian jewelry
designer Arielle De Pinto
(Fall-Winter 2012).

Cassina Vegetal Ebano Calf
Leather ankle boot with wedge heel
(Spring-Summer 2012).

Stuart Weitzman has gained ground as one of the leaders in the luxury footwear industry with his creations that blend design and comfort. His career began back in Haverhill, Massachusetts, where Stuart worked as an apprentice with his father, Seymour Weitzman in his shoe factory. In 1986, Stuart established his own luxury shoe company, which became a hobby as well as a business for him. Today Stuart Weitzman produces more than two million pairs of shoes per year, and the brand has presence in

STUART WEITZMAN

more than 70 countries all over the world. The secret of his success lies in meticulous design coupled with the craftsmanship of shoes handmade in Elda, Spain, where Stuart has his own factories. Each shoe passes through 200 artisans' hands during the seven-week manufacturing process, from the first sketch to the finished, boxed product. Weitzman believes that shoes must primarily serve one purpose: to dress women. For this reason, his designs are minuscule works of art, yet they never sacrifice comfort.

Stuart Weitzman's designs are minuscule works of art, yet they never sacrifice comfort.

The Million-Dollar Sandal

Silver sandal with 464 Swarovski crystals enveloping the foot in straps with a teardrop on the instep. Actress Laura Harring wore them at the 2002 Oscars, and a special edition was issued in 2012 to commemorate the 10th anniversary of this model.

Olivia Melon Flor Patent
Colorful strappy sandal
(Spring-Summer 2011).

Wizard of Oz

Red satin shoe with a large bow at the toe and peppered with Swarovski Elements from Swarovski Crystallized™. Commemoration of the 70th anniversary of the premier of *The Wizard of Oz* (2009).

Pipedagger
Fur print stiletto court shoe
(Fall-Winter 2012).

Lille

Cognac snakeskin print leather
court shoe with peep toe
(Fall-Winter 2010).

Uprise
Animal fur print court shoe
(Fall-Winter 2012).

Peppers
Satin model with gem-studded heel
(Spring-Summer 2009).

Heritage
Created to commemorate the company's 25th anniversary in the world of fashion (2011).

Timber

Black patent leather sandal with wooden platform and fake horn heel (Summer 2009).

Glotorrid

Precious black suede sandal with heel covered in Swarovski Elements (Fall-Winter 2009).

Holdfast
Imitation tortoiseshell Mary Jane
with metallic stiletto
(Winter 2012).

Stiletto

Court shoe created from iridescent fabric with gem-studded stiletto (Fall-Winter 2012).

Closecall

Black suede ankle boot with imitation
tortoiseshell trim and stiletto
(Fall-Winter 2012).

Middle
Red patent leather ankle boot
with metallic stiletto
(Fall-Winter 2012).

Lacemeup
Tall high-heeled leopard
print leather boot
(Fall-Winter 2010).

Pantalon
Leather boot
(Fall-Winter 2012).

The Trucco brand is based on the application of a highly personal lifestyle concept to fashion. How? By using design to interpret trends with comfort, elegance and quality. The brand's shoes are designed for a woman who requires a style suitable for a particular occasion, a real woman who likes to interpret fashion for herself, while seeking a touch of femininity and romanticism in the details. Trucco belongs to the Madrid-based Spanish manufacture and distribution company InSitu, which

TRUCCO

is exclusively responsible for designing, producing and marketing Trucco footwear. With more than 25 years of experience in the textile industry, Trucco has almost 200 points of sale all over the world, in places like Spain, Portugal, the Czech Republic, China, Saudi Arabia, Mexico, Qatar, Panama, Thailand, the Dominican Republic, Guatemala, Ecuador, Costa Rica and Iran. Its wide range of footwear is suitable for all kinds of events and women, ensuring that their feet are feminine as well as stylish.

*Trucco designs shoes for real women
who interpret fashion for themselves,
while seeking a touch of femininity
and romanticism in the details.*

Peep toe platform with metallic
stiletto secured at the instep with
a matching leather strap
(Fall-Winter 2012-2013).

Strappy sandal with ankle strap
(Spring-Summer 2011).

Burgundy leather court shoe
with brown heel and platform
(Fall-Winter 2010-2011).

Medium heel shoe with pointed toe
and green upper and heel
(Fall-Winter 2012-2013).

Dark brown snakeskin court shoe
with camel color back and heel
(Fall-Winter 2011-2012).

Suede court shoe in two-toned brown with high heel (Spring-Summer 2011).

Black suede high-heeled
sandal with ankle strap
(Fall-Winter 2011-2012).

Navy blue sandal with
ankle strap and medium heel
(Spring-Summer 2012).

Peep toe, lace-up ankle boot. The
brown wooden wedge contrasts
with the off-white suede of the shoe
(Spring-Summer 2012).

Off-white sandal with navy trim,
wooden wedge and back zip
(Spring-Summer 2012).

Plaited jute wedge with
elastic leather straps
(Spring-Summer 2011).

Gold leather sandal with block heel
(Spring-Summer 2012).

Lace-up chocolate brown suede ankle
boot with wooden heel and platform
(Fall-Winter 2011-2012).

Dark gray suede lace-up
ankle boot with block heel
(Fall-Winter 2010-2011).

Tall black suede boot with rubber sole
(Fall-Winter 2011-2012).

Fleece-lined waterproof rain boot with lambskin upper (Fall-Winter 2010-2011).

This story begins with a broken heart belonging to Dutch architect Rem Koolhaas. His frustration at being unable to get back together with his girlfriend was the catalyst that gradually shrunk his architecture to a smaller, more vulnerable scale—the size of a woman's foot. The result was the Möbius shoe. A short while later, Rem met Galahad Clark, a seventh generation member of the Clarks shoe dynasty. As soon as Galahad saw the design for the Möbius shoe at their meeting, without a second thought he partnered with Koolhaas to form United Nude in 2003. Since then, it has become an

UNITED NUDE

iconic brand at the crossroads between fashion and design. United Nude is, in fact, the result of the collaboration of a creative team comprised of architects, designers, editors and photographers. Their revolutionary designs constantly blur the boundaries between fashion, art, architecture and industrial design. Most surprisingly of all, the team draws inspiration from such dissimilar items—a chair, a tower, a building; whether it's an architectural structure or a single brick, it manages to challenge the laws of gravity.

United Nude blurs the boundaries between fashion, art, architecture and industrial design.

Eamz Pump

This bestseller pays tribute to architects Charles and Ray Eames and their famous Eames chair. The heel is suspended under an innovative shape (Spring-Summer 2012).

Lo Res
Court shoe designed using low-resolution computer software that enables the shoe to be converted into a polyhedral version with a metallic cast (Spring-Summer 2012).

Geisha
Japanese-inspired platform shoe
(Spring-Summer 2012).

Fold
Ankle boot made of a single strip
of fabric wrapped around the foot
front to back like a scarf
(Spring-Summer 2012).

Pin Naomi

Ankle boot with metallic pencil heel that combines materials such as leather and suede (Fall-Winter 2012-2013).

Block Pump

Model created based on a block, a squared structure that juts out from the back of the shoe. Designed as if they were two independent pieces, the heel and the upper are actually one single piece (Spring-Summer 2012).

Web

This model combines laser-cut leather with a metal wedge and slender heel, a construction that creates an optical illusion, resembling a column of air (Spring-Summer 2012).

Stealth Roman

Sandal inspired by the straight lines of the F-117 Stealth airplane. Base with straight lines wrought with mirror-like materials (Spring-Summer 2012).

Degrees

Sandal that combines materials such as leather, wood, rubber and carbon fiber. Its heel is at a 90° angle (Spring-Summer 2012).

Abstract Rome

Sandal with a heel comprising two connected wooden blocks that hold the leather upper, secured with tiny studs on the sides (Spring-Summer 2012).

The shoes of English designer Victoria Spruce are inspired by modern architecture, sculpture and futuristic design. Spruce studied shoe design at London's Cordwainers College, where she graduated in 2008. She later presented the shoe collection shown on these pages as her graduation project from the Royal College of Art in London, 2011. For now, Victoria does not have a footwear line per se; she only works on prototypes and one-off pieces, ensuring added value for the shoes she designs. Each

VICTORIA SPRUCE

of her works is a true sculpture, remarkable for its combination of hard materials and leather, as well as for its combination of new technologies and traditional techniques, resulting in shifting lines and curves that hug the feet. Inspired primarily by organic sculpture, her designs flow to create a continuous rhythm between shape and materials. There is no doubt that Victoria Spruce is an extraordinarily promising shoe designer who successfully blends fashion and art in each of her shoes.

*Victoria Spruce's shoes are remarkable
for their architectural and sculptural
lines with hints of futurism.*

Cut-out Wedge

Pale blue wedge sandal with plastic upper and leather-covered heel.

Contrast Sandal
Pale blue sandal with
leather upper and plastic toe.

Twisted Court

Nude court shoe with plastic upper and leather-covered heel.

Strappy Shoe-boot
Ankle boot with heel and platform
with leather upper with plastic straps.

Curvy Sling
Nude shoe with plastic heel and
platform and leather upper.

Curvy Heel Bootee

Off-white ankle boot with plastic heel and platform and leather upper.

Contrast Strappy
Sandal with plastic heel
and platform and leather upper.

2-Part Pump
Flat leather and plastic shoe.

The luxury brand Zoraide is a project launched in 2008 by Milanese-born Paola Bay, a contemporary art and haute-couture collector, film producer, fashion consultant and now designer. Zoraide's shoes, crafted with prized textiles and unique leathers, are targeted at women who seek perfection, exclusivity and simple luxury. Crafted by master Italian artisans, it takes two to four days to complete each model, creating truly limited editions. Each of Zoraide's creations pays special attention to detail, leathers and

ZORAIDE

design quality. Additionally, each collection is based on a specific theme such as disco divas, inspirational queens who defined an era, mythological figures and precious stones. The shoes are packaged in boxes designed specifically for each model and include a booklet designed by Chris Price and Delisia Howard, certifying them to be true works of art. This truly is the case: the shoes are now part of the permanent collection at the Galleria Museum of Paris, one of the most important museums in the fashion world.

Zoraide shoes, targeted at women who seek perfection, are crafted with prized textiles and unique leathers.

Irene

Pink velvet and silk court shoe with gold trim (Fall-Winter 2011-2012).

Rita
Pink napa sandal with upper comprising various leaf shapes (Spring-Summer 2013).

Donna

Lizard skin print embossed shoe,
a tribute to singer Donna Summer
(Spring-Summer 2012).

Holly
Silk shoe
(Spring-Summer 2012).

Salome
Reptile print high-heeled
shoe in red tones
(Fall-Winter 2011-2012).

Audrey
Silk shoe with felt flower inspired
by actress Audrey Hepburn
(Fall-Winter 2012-2013).

Debbie

Printed and embossed shoe with imitation diamond accessory (Spring-Summer 2012).

Neela
Leather and silk shoe
(Spring-Summer 2009).

Galatea

Gold and silver leather
sandal with high heel
(Spring-Summer 2008).

Laila
High-heeled silver leather sandal with suede flowers and imitation diamonds (Spring-Summer 2011).

Mary
Gold brocade crocodile print shoe
(Spring-Summer 2012).

Metis
Leather and brocade shoe
(Fall-Winter 2007-2008).

Adamoka
Green and silver leather shoe
(Fall-Winter 2010-2011).

Marilyn
Lizard print shoe inspired
by actress Marilyn Monroe
(Fall-Winter 2012-2013).

Gaspara
Black and silver leather shoe
(Fall-Winter 2009-2010).

Madonna

Black silk shoe embroidered with silver thread, worn by Madonna in her *Girl Gone Wild* video clip in 2012 (Fall-Winter 2012-2013).